A CHILD'S TREASURY OF
IRISH RHYMES

Barefoot Poetry Collections

an imprint of

Barefoot Books, Inc.

41 Schermerhorn Street, Suite 145

Brooklyn, New York

11201-4845

Compiled by Alice Taylor

Illustrations copyright © 1996 by Nicola Emoe

The moral right of Nicola Emoe to be identified as the illustrator of this work has been asserted

ISBN 1 902283 18 X

This book is printed on 100% acid-free paper

Graphic design by Design/Section

Printed and bound in Singapore by Tien Wah Press (Pte) Ltd

1 3 5 7 9 8 6 4 2

A CHILD'S TREASURY OF
IRISH RHYMES

Compiled by ALICE TAYLOR

Illustrated by NICOLA EMOE

BAREFOOT BOOKS

Contents

FOREWORD

Rhymes that we learn when we are very young stick to our minds like cream to the inside of a jug. They often come back unbidden in later life and cause a spurt of joy to shoot up in our hearts. They belong to carefree childhood days and enshrine within us a younger, more innocent edition of ourselves. That is why they are very special.

The rhymes collected here came to me in different ways. Fragments of some were printed faintly on the back pages of my mind but grew clearer as I tried to recall them. Others I had completely forgotten until a friend with better powers of recollection recited a lost line or two and then a locked door sprang open in my mind and the rest of the rhyme came tumbling out. "The Baby Over the Way" was one such rhyme; only when a friend of mine jogged my memory with the first line did I remember that perfect baby and how much I had disliked him.

The rhymes in this book take me back to my childhood; to the old farmhouse in rural Ireland where I learned some of them; and to the school in the fields where we would recite others line by line after the teacher so that by sheer dint of repetition they finally sank into our minds, never to be totally forgotten. Equally, when my father recited rhymes that he had learned at school, he would encompass me in the world of his childhood, building a bridge between the generations. In collecting these little rhymes for the very young I hope that another generation will be able to walk back over that bridge into another world, and that their parents and grandparents will walk with them.

Alice Taylor

THE FAIRIES

The fairies have never a penny to spend,
They haven't a thing put by,
But theirs is the dower of bird and of flower
And theirs are the earth and sky.
And though you should live in a palace of gold
Or sleep in a dried-up ditch,
You could never be poor as the fairies are,
And never as rich.

Since ever and ever the world began
They have danced like a ribbon of flame,
They have sung their song through the centuries long
And yet it is never the same.
And though you be foolish or though you be wise,
With hair of silver or gold,
You could never be young as the fairies are,
And never as old.

SAVING THE BACON

Thunder and lightning rent the air
And all the world was shaken,
The little pig cocked up his tail
And ran to save his bacon.

THE WHISPER-WHISPER MAN

The Whisper–Whisper Man
Makes all the wind in the world.
He has a gown as brown as brown:
His hair is long and curled.

In the stormy wintertime
He taps at your windowpane.
And all the night, until it's light,
He whispers through the rain.

If you peeped through a Fairy Ring
You'd see him, little and brown;
You'd hear the beat of his clackety feet
Scampering through the town.

9

THE PEDDLER'S CARAVAN

I wish I lived in a caravan,
With a horse to drive, like a peddler man!
Where he comes from nobody knows,
Or where he goes to, but on he goes.

His caravan has windows two,
And a chimney of tin, that the smoke comes through;
He has a wife and a baby brown,
And they go riding from town to town.

Chairs to mend, and delf' to sell!
He clashes the basins like a bell;
Tea-trays, baskets ranged in order,
Plates with the alphabet round the border.

The roads are brown, and the sea is green,
But his house is like a bathing machine;
The world is round, and he can ride,
Rumble and splash to the other side.

With the peddler man I should like to roam,
And write a book when I come home;
All the people would read my book,
Just like the Travels of Captain Cook.

LOST TIME

Timothy took his time to school,
Plenty of time he took;
But some he lost in the tadpole pool,
And some in the stickleback brook.
Ever so much in the linnet's nest,
And more on the five-bar gate –
Timothy took his time to school
But he lost it all and was late.

Timothy has a lot to do –
How shall it all be done?
Why, he has never got home till close on two,
Though he might have been home by one.
There's sums, and writing and spelling too;
And an apple tree to climb.
Timothy has a lot to do –
How shall he find the time?

Timothy sought it high and low:
He looked in the tadpole pool
To see if they'd taken the time to grow
That he lost on the way to school.

He found the nest, and he found the tree,
And he found the gate he crossed,
But Timothy never shall find (ah me!)
The time that Timothy lost.

THE THIN CAT

He walked upon our garden wall,
He hadn't got a home at all,
The thin cat, the thin cat,
The little homeless thin cat!

I don't believe he ever purred,
He never knew a loving word,
The thin cat, the thin cat,
The little homeless thin cat!

But Mother said, "Go bring him in,
I cannot bear to see him thin,"
The thin cat, the thin cat,
The little homeless thin cat!

So now he purrs upon the mat,
His coat is soft – he's warm and fat,
The fat cat, the fat cat,
The little happy fat cat!

MY SON HUGH

When the pipers' band comes down the street
(Playing Rum Tum Tum, playing Rum Tum Too),
The children follow with dancing feet,
And away with the rest goes my son Hugh.
Three feet four!
Not an inch more!
Away with the band goes my son Hugh.

He's so very, very small,
That he's hardly there at all,
And where does he march, think you?
The pipers come in line
Looking very fine
But they are not good enough for Hugh.
There's a big, big drummer man,

Ever so tall,
A big, big drummer,
The finest of them all;
Six feet high, and an inch or two to spare,
With his drum on his chest
And his head in the air –

He wears a skin
Of black and yellow
And marching by his side
Is a tiny little fellow.

Here they come
To the roll of the drum –
The big, big drummer man, six feet two,
And three foot four of my son Hugh.

THE BABY OVER THE WAY

The baby over the way I know
Is a better baby than me,
For the baby over the way is
All that a baby should be.
His frock is smooth, his bib is neat
And his ears are always clean,
He never wants a comforter or
Sips of tea from a spoon,
He never crumples his pinafore,
He never cries for the moon.
He's a dear little, sweet little angel bright,
A love and a dove, they say!
But when I grow up I'm going to fight
With the baby over the way.

THE IRISH STUDENT AND HIS CAT

I and Pangur Ban, my cat,
'Tis a like task we are at;
Hunting mice is his delight,
Hunting words I sit all night.

Better far than praise of men
'Tis to sit with book and pen;
Pangur bears me no ill will;
He, too, plies his simple skill.

'Tis a merry thing to see
At our task how glad are we,
When at home we sit and find
Entertainment to our mind.

Oftentimes a mouse will stray
Into the hero Pangur's way;
Oftentimes my keen thought set
Takes a meaning in its net.

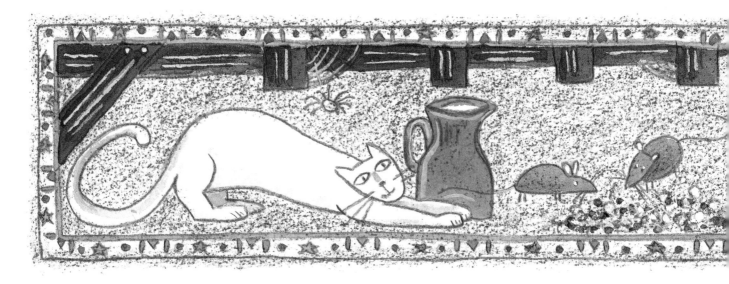

'Gainst the wall he sets his eye
Full and fierce and sharp and sly;
'Gainst the wall of knowledge I
All my little wisdom try.

When a mouse darts from its den,
O how glad is Pangur then!
O what gladness do I prove
When I solve the doubts I love!

So in peace our tasks we ply,
Pangur Ban, my cat, and I;
In our arts we find our bliss,
I have mine, and he has his.

Practice every day has made
Pangur perfect in his trade;
I get wisdom day and night,
Turning darkness into light.

MR NOBODY

I know a funny little man,
As quiet as a mouse,
Who does the mischief that is done
In everybody's house.
Though no one ever sees his face,
Yet we can all agree
That every plate we break was cracked
By Mr Nobody.

'Tis he who always tears our books,
Who leaves the door ajar,
Who pulls the buttons from our shirts,
And scatters pins afar.
That squeaking door will always squeak
For – this is plain to see –
We leave the oiling to be done
By Mr Nobody.

'Tis he who brings in all the mud
That gathers in the hall.
'Tis he who lets the front door slam,
And scribbles on the wall.
When we can't find the scissors,
Or have lost the back door key,
The one to blame in every case
Is Mr Nobody.

We know he cracked the window
And broke the china plate,
We know he left the kitchen floor
In such a dreadful state.
We know his faults and failings,
His sins are plain to see,
And so we always put the blame
On Mr Nobody.

BIRD THOUGHTS

I lived once in a little house
And lived there very well;
I thought the world was small and round,
And made of pale-blue shell.

I lived next in a little nest,
Nor needed any other;
I thought the world was made of straw,
And builded by my mother.

One day I flew down from the nest
To see what I could find,
"The world is made of leaves," I said;
"I have been very blind."

And then I flew beyond the tree,
Quite fit for grown-up labors;
I don't know how the world is made
And neither do my neighbors.

MICHAEL MET A WHITE DUCK

Michael met a white duck
Walking on the green:
"How are you?" said Michael.
"How fine the weather's been!
Blue sky and sunshine,
All through the day:
Not a single raindrop
Came to spoil our play."

But the sad white duck said,
"I myself want rain,
I'd like to see the brooklets
And the streams fill up again.
Now I can't go swimming,
It really makes me cry
To see the little duckponds
Look so very dry."

THE LITTLE ELF MAN

I saw a little elf man once,
Down where the lilies blow.
I asked him why he was so small,
And why he didn't grow.

He slightly frowned, and with his eye
He looked me through and through.
"I'm quite as big for me," said he,
"As you are big for you."

THE FAIRY SHOEMAKER

I caught him at work one day, myself,
In the castle ditch, where foxglove grows –
A wrinkled, wizened and bearded elf,
Spectacles stuck on his pointed nose,
Silver buckles on his hose.

The rogue was mine without a doubt,
I stared at him; he stared at me;
"Servant, Sir!" "Humph!" says he,
And pulled a snuffbox out.
He took a long pinch, looked better pleased,
The queer little Leprechaun;
Offered the box with whimsical grace –
Pouf! he flung the dust in my face,
And, while I sneezed,
Was gone!

THE LITTLE DONKEY

I saw a donkey
One day old,
His head was too big
For his neck to hold.

His legs were shaky
And long and loose,
They rocked and staggered
And weren't much use.

He tried to gambol
And frisk a bit,
But he wasn't sure
Of the trick of it.

His queer little coat
Was soft and grey,
And curled at his neck
In a lovely way.

His face was wistful,
And left no doubt
That he felt life needed
Some thinking out.

So he blundered round
In venturous quest,
And then lay flat
On the ground to rest.

He looked so little
And weak and slim,
I prayed the world
Might be good to him.

THE BALLAD SINGER

She sang in Wexford town
In the little crooked street;
I was thinking of the beauty
Of her small brown feet.

Her voice was like the wind
That wails on All Souls' Night;
She sang from door to door
In the waning light.

She stretched a timid hand
For pennies that I gave;
A sadness in her eyes
Deeper than the grave.

She sang a ballad of Wexford
In the empty marketplace;
I thought of the Mother of God
And the sorrow on Her face.

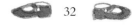

THE WOOD OF FLOWERS

I went to the Wood of Flowers,
No one went with me;
I was there alone for hours;
I was happy as could be,
In the Wood of Flowers!

There was grass
On the ground;
There were leaves
On the trees;

And the wind
Had a sound
Of such sheer
Gaiety;

That I
Was as happy
As happy could be,
In the Wood of Flowers.

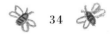

THE "GOOD PEOPLE"

From our hidden places
By a secret path
We troop in the moonlight
To the edge of the green rath.

There the night through
We take our pleasure
Dancing to such measure
As earth never knew.

HAPPY APPLE

If I were an apple and grew on a tree,
I think I'd fall down on a nice boy like me;
I wouldn't stay there giving nobody joy,
I'd fall down at once and say; "Eat me, my boy."

THE GARDEN GRASS

This is a thing that I can't understand,
Which I can't understand or explain –
No matter how often we cut the grass
It keeps coming up again.

It keeps coming up through the holes in the ground,
No matter how often we mow –
There must be miles and miles of grass
Coiled up down below.

Dad says that the worms are winding it there,
And that that's why it never can stop
Coming out through the holes in the lid of the earth –
Like the twine in Dan Hegarthy's shop.

OCTOBER'S PARTY

October gave a party;
The leaves in hundreds came –
The Chestnuts, Oaks and Maples,
The leaves of every name.

The sunshine spread a carpet,
And everything was grand,
Miss Weather led the dancing,
Professor Wind the band.

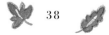

The Chestnuts came in Yellow,
The Oaks in crimson dressed;
The lovely Missus Maple
In scarlet looked her best.

All balanced to their partners,
And gaily fluttered by,
The sight was like a rainbow
New fallen from the sky.

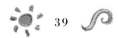

AN OLD WOMAN OF THE ROADS

Oh, to have a little house!
To own the hearth and stool and all!
The heaped-up sods upon the fire,
The pile of turf against the wall!

To have a clock with weights and chains
And pendulum swinging up and down,
A dresser filled with shining delf',
Speckled and white and blue and brown!

I could be busy all the day
Clearing and sweeping hearth and floor,
And fixing on their shelf again
My white and blue and speckled store!

I could be quiet there at night
Beside the fire and by myself,
Sure of a bed and loth to leave
The ticking clock and shining delf'!

Och! but I'm weary of mist and dark,
And roads where there's never a house nor bush,
And tired I am of bog and road
And the crying wind and the lonesome hush!

And I am praying to God on high,
And I am praying Him night and day,
For a little house, a house of my own,
Out of the wind's and the rain's way.

A NEW YEAR CALL

A fairy came to call me
At twilight time today.
He coasted down an icicle,
But said he couldn't stay
For more than sixty-seven blinks
To Happy-New-Year me;
And wouldn't take his mittens off
For he had had his tea.

He sat upon the window-sill,
His wings all puckered in,
And talked about the New Year deeds
He thought he would begin;
He said he'd help the fairies more
And birds and flower folk;
He'd teach the kittens how to purr
And baby frogs to croak.

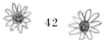

This year, he said, he'd practice up
His fairy scales and sing
The woodland world all wide awake
By twenty winks to Spring;
He'd never tease the butterflies,
Nor the whip-poor-wills,
But he would feed the daisies dew
And dust the daffodils.

And he would mind his fairy queen
For years and years and years,
And wear his rubbers when he should
And wash behind his ears.
He perked his wings up then, and winked
And sang a goodbye tune,
Then left a snowflake calling-card
And flew up to the moon.

A CHILD'S EVENSONG

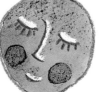

The sun is weary, for he ran
So far and fast today;
The birds are weary, for who sang
So many songs as they?
The bees and butterflies at last
Are tired out, for just think, too,
How many gardens through the day
Their little wings have fluttered through.

And so, as all tired people do,
They've gone to lay their sleepy heads,
Deep, deep in warm and happy beds.

The sun has shut his golden eye
And gone to sleep beneath the sky;
The birds and butterflies and bees
Have all crept into flowers and trees,
And all lie quiet, and still as mice,
Till morning comes.

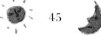

A Cradle Song

O men from the fields,
Come softly within!
Tread softly, softly,
O men coming in!

Mavourneen is going
From me and from you,
Where Mary will fold him
With mantle of blue!

From reek of the smoke
And cold of the floor,
And the peering of things
Across the half-door.

O men from the fields,
Softly, softly come thro'!
Mary puts round him
Her mantle of blue.

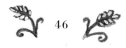

A Prayer

Father, we thank you for the night,
And for the pleasant morning light,
For the rest and food and loving care,
And all that makes the world more fair.

Help us to do the things we should,
To be to others kind and good,
In all we do, in all we say,
To grow more loving every day.

ACKNOWLEDGMENTS

Rhymes with attributed authors are listed in
order of appearance; all other entries are anonymous:

"The Fairies" by Rose Fyleman; "The Peddler's Caravan" by
W.B. Rands; "Lost Time" by Ffrida Wolfe; "The Thin Cat" by
Florence Hoatsom; "My Son Hugh" by John Desmond Sheridan,
copyright © by John Desmond Sheridan, reproduced by kind permission of
John P. Sheridan; "Michael Met a White Duck" by J. Dupuy; "The Little Elf Man"
by John K. Bangs; "The Fairy Shoemaker" by William Allingham; "The Little
Donkey" by Elizabeth Shane; "The Ballad Singer" by M. J. MacManus; "The
Wood of Flowers" by James Stephens, copyright © by James Stephens, reproduced
by kind permission of the Society of Authors as the literary representative of James
Stephens; "The 'Good People'" by Seamus O'Sullivan; "The Garden Grass" by
John Desmond Sheridan, copyright © by John Desmond Sheridan, reproduced by
kind permission of John P. Sheridan; "October's Party" by George Cooper; "An
Old Woman of the Roads" by Padraic Colum, copyright © by Padraic Colum,
reproduced by kind permission of Maire Colum O'Sullivan; "A New Year Call"
by Marjorie Barrows; "A Child's Evensong" by R. Le Galliene; "A Cradle Song"
by Padraic Colum, copyright © by Padraic Colum, reproduced by kind permission
of Maire Colum O'Sullivan.

The publishers have made every effort to contact holders of copyright material.
If you have not received our correspondence, please contact us for inclusion in
future editions.

BAREFOOT BOOKS publishes high-quality picture books for children of all ages and specializes in the work of artists and writers from many cultures. If you have enjoyed this book and would like to receive a copy of our current catalog, please write to our New York office: Barefoot Books, 41 Schermerhorn Street, Suite 145, Brooklyn, New York, NY 11201-4845 email: ussales@barefoot-books.com website: www.barefoot-books.com